DATE DUE

SAFETY/LA SEGURIDAD
FIRST/ES LO PRIMERO

Staying Safe / La seguridad
On the School Bus / en el autobús escolar

by/por Joanne Mattern

Reading consultant/Consultora de lectura: Susan Nations, M.Ed.,
author, literacy coach, consultant in literacy development/
autora, tutora de alfabetización, consultora de desarrollo de la lectura

Please visit our web site at: www.garethstevens.com
For a free color catalog describing **Weekly Reader**® **Early Learning Library's list**
of high-quality books, call 1-877-445-5824 (USA) or 1-800-387-3178 (Canada).
Weekly Reader® **Early Learning Library's fax: (414) 336-0164.**

Library of Congress Cataloging-in-Publication Data

Mattern, Joanne, 1963-
    [Staying safe on the school bus. Spanish & English]
    Staying safe on the school bus = la seguridad en el autobús escolar / by Joanne Mattern.
        p. cm. — (Safety first / La seguridad es lo primero)
    Includes bibliographical references and index.
    ISBN-13: 978-0-8368-8060-1 (lib. bdg.)
    ISBN-13: 978-0-8368-8067-0 (softcover)
    1. School children—Transportation—Safety measures—Juvenile literature.
    2. School buses—Safety measures—Juvenile literature.   3. Safety education—Juvenile literature.
    I. Title.   II. Title: Seguridad en el autobús escolar.
    LB2864.M3512   2007
    363.12'59—dc22
                                                                              2006035348

This edition first published in 2007 by
Weekly Reader® **Early Learning Library**
A Member of the WRC Media Family of Companies
330 West Olive Street, Suite 100
Milwaukee, WI 53212 USA

Copyright © 2007 by Weekly Reader® Early Learning Library

Managing editor: Valerie J. Weber
Editor: Barbara Kiely Miller
Art direction: Tammy West
Cover design and page layout: Charlie Dahl
Picture research: Diane Laska-Swanke
Photographer: Jack Long
Spanish translation: Tatiana Acosta and Guillermo Gutiérrez

The publisher thanks Sage and Judi Austin, Josie, Daniel Burss, Tyler Cartagena, Christopher Ginter, Michael
Hanke, Christina Kingsawan, Amber and Tayler Kozelek, Maria Najera, Rubie Rowe, Temple Woods,
Lukas and Maria Zabel, Garrett Bennett, Tammy Janichek, Patty Raschig, and Riteway Bus Service for their
assistance with this book.

Printed in the United States of America

1 2 3 4 5 6 7 8 9 10 10 09 08 07 06

Note to Educators and Parents

Reading is such an exciting adventure for young children! They are beginning to integrate their oral language skills with written language. To encourage children along the path to early literacy, books must be colorful, engaging, and interesting; they should invite the young reader to explore both the print and the pictures.

The *Safety First* series is designed to help young readers review basic safety rules, learn new vocabulary, and strengthen their reading comprehension. In simple, easy-to-read language, each book teaches children to stay safe in an everyday situation such as at home, school, or in the outside world.

Each book is specially designed to support the young reader in the reading process. The familiar topics are appealing to young children and invite them to read — and reread — again and again. The full-color photographs and enhanced text further support the student during the reading process.

In addition to serving as wonderful picture books in schools, libraries, homes, and other places where children learn to love reading, these books are specifically intended to be read within an instructional guided reading group. This small group setting allows beginning readers to work with a fluent adult model as they make meaning from the text. After children develop fluency with the text and content, the book can be read independently. Children and adults alike will find these books supportive, engaging, and fun!

— Susan Nations, M.Ed., author/literacy coach/
and consultant in literacy development

Nota para los maestros y los padres

¡Leer es una aventura tan emocionante para los niños pequeños! A esta edad están comenzando a integrar su manejo del lenguaje oral con el lenguaje escrito. Para animar a los niños en el camino de la lectura incipiente, los libros deben ser coloridos, estimulantes e interesantes; deben invitar a los jóvenes lectores a explorar la letra impresa y las ilustraciones.

La seguridad es lo primero es una nueva colección diseñada para ayudar a los jóvenes lectores a repasar normas de seguridad básicas, aprender vocabulario nuevo y reforzar su comprensión de la lectura. Con un lenguaje sencillo y fácil de leer, cada libro enseña a los niños cómo estar seguros en situaciones de la vida diaria en casa, la escuela o cuando salen de paseo.

Cada libro está especialmente diseñado para ayudar a los jóvenes lectores en el proceso de lectura. Los temas familiares llaman la atención de los niños y los invitan a leer una y otra vez. Las fotografías a todo color y el tamaño de la letra ayudan aún más al estudiante en el proceso de lectura.

Además de servir como maravillosos libros ilustrados en escuelas, bibliotecas, hogares y otros lugares donde los niños aprenden a amar la lectura, estos libros han sido especialmente concebidos para ser leídos en un grupo de lectura guiada. Este contexto permite que los lectores incipientes trabajen con un adulto que domina la lectura mientras van determinando el significado del texto. Una vez que los niños dominan el texto y el contenido, el libro puede ser leído de manera independiente. ¡Estos libros les resultarán útiles, estimulantes y divertidos a niños y a adultos por igual!

— Susan Nations, M.Ed., autora/tutora de
alfabetización/consultora de desarrollo de la lectura

Here comes the school bus!
Let's learn to ride safely.

¡Ahí viene el autobús escolar!
Vamos a aprender cómo ir
en autobús con seguridad.

Wait for the bus on the **sidewalk** or grass.

- - - - - - - - - - - - - -

Espera al autobús en la **acera** o sobre el pasto.

sidewalk/acera

7

Make sure the bus stops before you go near it. Hold on to the **handrail**. Walk slowly up the steps.

- - - - - - - - - - - - - - -

Antes de acercarte, asegúrate de que el autobús está parado. Agárrate del **pasamanos**. Sube los escalones despacio.

handrail/pasamanos

9

Pick a seat and stay seated.

--- --- --- --- --- --- --- --- --- --- --- ---

Elige un asiento y quédate allí.

11

Keep your head and hands inside the bus.

- - - - - - - - - - - -

No saques la cabeza ni las manos por la ventanilla.

Help the bus **driver** keep you safe. Do not shout or throw things in the bus.

— — — — — — — — — — — — —

Ayuda al **conductor** a mantener la seguridad. No grites ni tires cosas en el autobús.

FIRE EXTINGUISHER INSIDE

MAX. CAP. 71

Time to get off! Make sure your stuff does not get caught on the bus.

¡Es hora de bajar! Asegúrate de que tus cosas no se enganchan dentro del autobús.

Walk away from the bus
carefully. The driver must
be able to see you go.

- - - - - - - - - - - - -

Aléjate del autobús con
precaución. Hazlo de manera
que el conductor pueda verte.

Wait for cars to stop before you cross the street. Have a safe bus trip every day!

- - - - - - - - - - - - - - -

Antes de cruzar la calle, espera a que los autos se paren. ¡Que tu viaje en autobús sea seguro todos los días!

Glossary

alarm — a sound, light, or other signal that warns people about danger

bullies — people who are mean to other people or who try to hurt them

fire drill — the practice of the right way to get out of a building in case of a fire

practice — to repeat something many times so you can get better at it

recess — a short time to rest or play during the day

Glosario

alarma — sonido, luz u otra señal que advierte a las personas del peligro

niños abusivos — niños que se comportan mal con los demás o que tratan de hacerles daño

practicar — hacer algo varias veces para mejorar

recreo — periodo corto del día para descansar o jugar

simulacro de incendio — práctica de la manera correcta de salir de un edificio en caso de incendio

For More Information/Más información

Books/Libros

Autobuses escolares. Transportes (series). Dee Ready (Bridgestone Books)

Bus Driver/El conductor del autobús. People in My Community/La gente de mi comunidad (series). Jacqueline Laks Gorman (Gareth Stevens Publishing)

Choferes de autobuses escolares. Servidores Comunitarios (series). Dee Ready (Bridgestone books)

En autobús. ¡Vámonos! (series). Susan Ashley (Gareth Stevens Publishing)

Hello, School Bus! Marjorie Blain Parker (Cartwheel)

My School Bus: A Book About School Bus Safety. My World (series). Heather L. Feldman (PowerKids Press)

Index

Índice

About the Author

Joanne Mattern has written more than 150 books for children. She has written about weird animals, sports, world cities, dinosaurs, and many other subjects. Joanne also works in her local library. She lives in New York State with her husband, three daughters, and assorted pets. She enjoys animals, music, going to baseball games, reading, and visiting schools to talk about her books.

Información sobre la autora

Joanne Mattern ha escrito más de ciento cincuenta libros para niños. Ha escrito textos sobre animales extraños, deportes, ciudades del mundo, dinosaurios y muchos otros temas. Además, Joanne trabaja en la biblioteca de su comunidad. Vive en el estado de Nueva York con su esposo, sus tres hijas y varias mascotas. A Joanne le gustan los animales, la música, ir al béisbol, leer y hacer visitas a las escuelas para hablar de sus libros.